FEATHERWEIGHT

I am a feather for each wind that blows
– William Shakespeare

Remembering Nicholas Treacy

Noelle Lynskey

FEATHERWEIGHT

ARLEN
HOUSE

Featherweight

is published in 2025 by
ARLEN HOUSE
42 Grange Abbey Road
Baldoyle, Dublin 13, Ireland
Phone: 00 353 86 8360236
arlenhouse@gmail.com
arlenhouse.com

978–1–85132–341–8, *paperback*

Distributed internationally by
SYRACUSE UNIVERSITY PRESS
621 Skytop Road, Suite 110
Syracuse, New York 13244–5290
United States
Phone: 315–443–5534
supress@syr.edu
syracuseuniversitypress.syr.edu

Typesetting by Arlen House

cover images:
'Music Score' by Patrick Real
'Which Came First' by Joyce Soden
are reproduced courtesy of the artists

Contents

to the memory of my parents
James Lynskey and Frances Morrison

FEATHERWEIGHT

RED SQUIRREL DAYS

On red squirrel days I am lighter in the world,
or maybe the world is lighter on me,
no weight of missing out on blackberry time
or guilt of failed-to-set-gooseberry-days
or my should-have-got-up-earlier-dawns.

On I-wish-I'd-never-got-up kind of days
I set my gaze skyward, scale the heights,
snap the freedom of my red squirrel ways,
take a leap and trust my landing will hold
for the far-too-often-humdrum-days.

On red squirrel days, alert and bushy tailed,
balanced on any branch, eyes tilted to the sun,
I believe I can bear the heft of my burdens,
stash acorns of rhymes in the well of my drey
and pen lines to thrill the tufts of your ears.

SUNDAY RITUAL

From the door of their small shop
that opened into the back room, I watched
the soaping of his shiny apple head,
uncapped only on Sunday mornings,
herself leaning over the kitchen sink
in her ritual, as personal
as a whispered prayer.

My wonder at the sight of a wife
washing a man's face,
her hands circled in bubbles
cupping the water to rinse the week away,
then shave his stubble in sandy strokes,
the kettle boiling on the Rayburn,
two eggs poaching,
his gleaming face renewed.

Only the wheeze from their red shop door
lured me away
to serve at the counter,
witness to an intimacy
I couldn't fathom at eleven.

Their comfort with my presence
steadily drew me in to share their table,
taste my first salted island of yellow yolk
set in a shining sea of white.

My first glimpse
of the comfort of a poached egg,
of a woman so loving,
of a man so naked, so loved.

WHITE OWL'S FEATHER

His patience proven by the way he waited,
his love by the way he heeded,
hands that minded her, watched for her,
to talk, sleep or simply smile for him;
the tender way he had of draping the towel
over the clotheshorse, his fatherly coaxing
of her baby curls after she was bathed;
their two heads shadow-playing in the sun
while side by side they settled
on the windowsill, their chirrup of rhymes
like a pair of sparrows;
up the airy mountain,
down the rushy glen,
before that December night when a truck
on a bend threw his car at an angle,
his watching ended, her childhood over,
just a week short of her tenth birthday.

She finds herself lost between
the caw of the mourning crow
and the heft of a night owl, too young
to clench her sorrow with its name,
too old not to grasp its silence, yet
she hears his lilt of tongue
and turn of language:
trooping all together
in his chair, an old car seat shaped for him
from somewhere she never knew;
and white owl's feather
floating away there over the range
where the lamb shank squeaked
in the pot on the hearth.

She retraces the swirls on the buttons of his Garda coat,
nuzzles on the bobbles of his sea-blue jumper.

CONFESSION TO MY FATHER

The day we buried you I was discovered
there in your shed, among your stacks of turf,
timber, old tea chests full of tools, spare
valves, bulbs and plugs and other daddy stuff.

Why my mother came out to the backyard
I'll never know. Our house, bewildered
with ham eaters, pot scrubbers, bread slicers,
whiskey drinkers, familiar voices and faces
I barely knew. Maybe she was escaping too,
running away from the sympathy, the pity,
the crushing handshakes.

Those slender gift boxes of Silk Cut and Carroll's
lying among the sliced loaves and borrowed glasses
were just too tempting for the nine-year-old me.
Armed with matches, my ten-year-old neighbour
and a fistful of cigarettes, there
in your shed we choked ourselves on smoke.

I don't remember
the airiness in my head,
our lungs drowning in the fumes,
the guilty stifled giggles
and suppressed cough.

But I do hear
my mother's voice, suffering in those new shoes
that were killing her. There in her black dress,
eyes on fire,

That's all I need.

Not to be Contained

Sure, you'll only be scalded by nettles,
my mother warned, sensing the restlessness
in my long legs;
                    fuelled by the fire
of being twelve years old,
                    my longing to swish
and swerve through tall grass
there   beyond the edge
of the hard hopscotched tarmacadam;
                    unaware,
how unsure my footing might be through the ridges
of meadows or the barbs of sheep wire
                    until the day I did.

With one shoe   lost,
buried in the marsh beyond,
I hobbled home,
                    with that same gut wrench,
that dread of closing my little-girl eyes
for fear of the bogey man
stealing my mother away;
                         after all
he did take my father from me.

LEAVING HOME

There he is!
Timid and scared,
yet leaps with taught faith

out of the long grass;
his bushy tail
overwhelming

his skinny youth.
When he vaults over the dog
to shimmy up the tree

you could almost touch
his red fur as he sweeps
past, eyes fastened upwards,

ears fixed and alert,
the cliff of bark his lifeline.
Sharply he ascends,

grapples to the top branch –
clinging to its sway
or to his own quiver.

Somewhere out of sight
a mother eyes her son
and sighs;
his father
regards his single act
with quiet satisfaction.

BROWN COATS
for Mary Barry

I am one of two brown coats
stepping off the No 11 bus
(about to get familiar with each other).
I check out the style of the other:
more waisted, a lighter shade of chestnut,
just as sensible as me however,
chosen maternally
by two practical mothers, sending
their 17 year olds to the big city,
cloaked in cloth guaranteed
to protect from the rain,
the cold. We are drawn together.

From the bus stop
heading to Front Gate
earthed by the familiar waft
from Peterson's tobacco shop
my pocket promises to carry
a quarter back home to Pat,
the neighbour in my left-behind town,
bald head, fingers tanned with years
of rolling Condor Plug.

Side by side, us coats
hang out together, over chairs,
inside lockers, on carriers of bikes.
Two sets of saucer eyes
discover the new geographies
of Front Square, the Pav,
the Cumberland, St Mark's,
trying to make a home of elsewhere,
its strange bustle and stream of bus routes.
Comforted by our uniformity
the tone of the bog

the same shade as the coat.
The return weekend train to the city
flits by familiar fields,
station names like nursery rhymes,
Boyle, Ballymote,
Mullingar, Maynooth,
as loneliness like an autumn scarf
weaves into the pair of coats. Drawing us closer
we unbutton the differences in each other,
delve into the lining of our lives.

We flaunt in the safety
of two, like Edna O'Brien's *Country Girls*,
sleeve in sleeve, seldom seen apart,
shoulder pads well tested
as an only child in gabardine
is glad to have the lapel of another.
So many chats are sown into our seams,
so many secrets are under the collar
and a world walked in matching good shoes.

In time we wear ourselves out,
move from bicycle to car,
flat to house and apart,
outgrowing the worn weave
of two brown coats
left behind.

A PHOTO OF MY MOTHER IN MAYO

Your arms at rest on the red half-door,
closed, yet open, you're half-in, half-out
facing the glare of the May sun and crows,
your arms both rest on the red half-door
of the threshold you stepped through some four
decades past, a place you seldom spoke about.
Your arms rest over that red half-door,
closed, still open, half-in-half-out.

WAYLAID IN THE GRAVEYARD

You lean in over the wall watching your mother
weave among the mourners,
her hand out to neighbours she grew up with,
embracing some, a few words
for all. When the air resounds with spades
she makes her way in your direction,
knowing you will be close enough to the car,
parked near the toilet, the place
she visits last. You follow her routine.
She marks every season of roses and heathers,
comments on the gaudy wreaths,
tracks fresh clay piles
and new inscriptions on familiar headstones.

When the mourners scatter, you see her
head towards you. She'll be
one of the last to leave. Inside the gate,
to the left, lie your grandparents.
You join her there as she blesses herself,
you respond as she recites another decade.
She's so at home on this burial ground,
between the bones of Morrison's and Davey's,
close to the homes of Ryan's and Looby's
in townlands from Aghanagh to Bricklieve,
Heapstown to Kilmactranny.
All to be repeated on the reverse journey,
a mantra you will recite yourself
long after she's waylaid herself.

HER STILLNESS
after Sharon Olds

Do you think am I dying? she whispers.
We wait. He pauses.

When the doctor says to our mother, "We will
make you as comfortable as we can," the room inhales
the weight of his reply.

She lies quietly,
her lips shaping her prayers. We are lost,
orphaned already.

The doctor slips out.
My sisters read hope from his words,
patting her pillow, soothing
the woman who lullabied our lives.

Our brother, unreadable as ever, leans closer.
No comfort now in this stark space. The sparse
room a mirror of his solitude.

And I, I do what I can only do.
I hold her hand. The bruised
tissue of her skin already giving in.

Her eyes focus on each of us. One by one,
she gives a nod. In a final wave
she raises my hand to her lips
in a tender brush. Together,
we hold her
breath.

A Journey's Yarns and Strands

I

Daylight falls differently, new shadows
steal around the silence. Stranded, I reach across
the empty seat where your body once curved.

Shielding yourself from the windscreen's glare
you'd root out your tinted pair of glasses
from the handbag used for those journeys

where money for a stop at the Royal Hotel
was stashed with the hanky and rosary beads,
your blessing from Knock. On your weekly drive

down familiar roads you carried me as a child
in the green Ford Anglia, round curves,
bends and through crossroads until we arrived

at your mother's, where you and my generous
granny drew us to the mystery of salt air
and sand dunes by the cannon at Strandhill.

Evenings over plates of ham, the easy banter
of generations, my dress gathering
crumbs of her Jacob's Chocolate Goldgrain

as the chat of women resonated over the range:
the shades of yarn for the lastest cardigan,
the price of Clark's shoes in Connolly's,

the latest hearsay from Kilmorgan, the clank
of the bucket from Clare's well as it refilled
the broad bellied kettle for the next pot.

Heading back home over the purple Curlews,
every whin bush had its yellow tale
as I browned my face with Scots Clan,

counted silver stars and pearl Hail Marys
as decade after decade was recited over and over
delivering us from Boyle to our own front door.

II

For you, my life weaver and yarn stitcher,
today's visit is a new pilgrimage,

scattered with strands of you.
I drive alone,

stand at stones engraved with dates,
familiar patterns in my backstory.

I draw the seat belt now
through your absence.

My map is missing.

REELING HER IN

When my grandmother looked into my mother's eyes,
she saw what I see in my daughter's.

– Vona Groarke

She bends down, despite her creaking limbs,
gathering the heap of envelopes in the post.
The soft square package stands out from the rest,
its obvious thickness stirs her curious mind.
Straightening up, a little stooped by joints
that keep her in check, even on her 80th birthday.

She sits at the kitchen table, perusing the envelopes,
her astute eye spotting a familiar hand,
her sister, her daughter, a childlike scrawl of a grandchild,
stamps from London, Paris and as far as Singapore.
Opening the cards, the signatures scanned,
each verse, each wish fills her with delight.

Leaving the packaged gift to last,
she falters, her once nimble fingers
tremble as she unveils the contents.
It's a CD, the newfangled LP.
From the cover, faces smile up at her.
She names the musicians, most from the past,

lists the chosen tunes that make her feet tap
with notes and trills that course her veins
since the day she was born. She couldn't miss.
Slipping the disc into the player on her dresser,
power on, volume up, her silent kitchen
is transformed, her feet treble to the beat,

swishing her back to Keash on Garland Sunday.
Her hair curled, costume on, she's dancing a jig
on the mountainside; Tommy Flynn reeling her in.

Reeling her back to the stout and tobacco days,
murmurs of the men filing in to a seat, and a swig
near the tunes, her father's bow spiralling

his magic. Her mother's big teapot pouring along
the bench, a gap made on the cold floor for her little feet
among the hobnails; the leap, the sweat, the breath,
the cold of the water from the outside bucket drowning
the moon. She drank a mug of stars those nights.
Here in her kitchen, she dances the lead round, the side step.

Heel turn, toe flick, the twirling disc and dancer, reel
after reel: *The Sky Lark, Sligo Maid,*
Bonnie Kate, Miss McCloud's, Knotted Chord
Pinch of Snuff, Moving Bog, Bunch of Keys.
Her swollen knees and purple knots of veins
pulse out back, then back 2 3 4.
She's a mayfly hovering over Lough Arrow.
Her father fiddles from his butter box in the corner,
smiling flakes of rosin from his Sligo strings.

The tunes end, her feet stall and she slows
down, the pulse beating so hard in her ear
she swears it's his hands playing the kettle
drum. She checks in the corner but he's gone.
It's her own heart thrumming in her head.

Slowly, removing the CD from the player,
she wipes the sweat from her forehead,
the CD's shiny surface mirrors her flushed cheeks,
her breathless mouth, furrowed wrinkles
beneath her eyes. Those eyes. They glint,
those eyes of childhood. Delighted,
she sits back, smiles, realising
her granddaughter has her sparkling eyes.

Her heartbeat drums away, the same heart
that's hummed each day, that danced at every
crossroad and on every flagstone
from Boyle to Ballymote.

Happy birthday indeed.

MEMORARE*

Perhaps it was the murmur,
the hum of the memorare,
a familiar click of bone and bead,

or the way the word *remember*
rounded itself in a whisper
in my one dream since your death

that, after an orphaned year
bookended in mourning,
my caged grief caved in.

For it could only be your lips
that left that scent of rosary
at the tip of my sleep-filled rest,

that same music of our ascent
on the journeys from Ballyrush
over the Curlews,

as I counted stars
you – the glorious mysteries.

* *Memorare: from the Latin 'Remember' is a Roman Catholic prayer to
the Blessed Virgin Mary.*

HOPE IS THE THING
after Emily Dickinson

In your wake a daily flurry
of feathers fall, pure white
handfuls of angel gifts,
to light and guard,

sprinkled wingfalls from above
land on the green grass
light as silky snowflakes,
to rule and guide.

Cleaved into a patio crack
a lone quill
stands

a nudge of hope
to inspire
a dip down my wordwell.

STILL BORN
for Síofra

She whispers my name often,
the one she gave me after.

No one hears but the worn Jesus
on the swinging crucifix
of her fingered beads.

Fingers that wound the wool,
one plain, one purl,
for the promise of me.

She stitched my shape into cardigans
I'd never wear,
buttonholes my eyes peeped through
in her nightly dreams.

I never was. Just
slipped into her waiting arms
with the cold absence of sound.

In some deep recess of her loss,
her name for me nestles in her throat.

Shadows play games with her.
Sometimes I skip like a dropped stitch
across the flapping screen
of her washed-out bloody sheets,

loss her repeating pattern:
each cycle, each moon, each year.

Her cry, the only cry.
Born still but still born,
an almost.

HEIRLOOM

a souvenir of stranded wisps,
your chestnut hair
posing on the bathroom tiles

steamed in curlicues
or cast from your brush
like a skein of yarn

is a windborne promise
to line a nest of bird dreams
with abandoned curls

of careless teenage art
swept upwards
like a double helix

coils that frame your face
your inescapable gene

the elegant poise
of your dead grandmother.

SEASONING

August a month of slowness,
lazy wasps hang about,
blackberries brushing green to red.

It catches you – the sideways sun
peppering the lush thickets –
then the rush

back to school before
the month has turned
herself over to the 1st.

No break to pick the ripe berries,
to lick their purple
gleam before the jar is sealed.

No time to stay up late,
bathe in the silver night,
the harvest moon.

The last chance of a dip
in the chilly salt of sea
and vinegared chips, missed.

What hurry is on them?
Let them off
for a few days more,

see them grow
another inch.

PUTTING A SHAPE ON THINGS

Late August her bigger-than-baby
steps make a colourful splash
on pavements of paper

in her hand-me-down red top,
vowels round up in search
of syllables, her head a playground

of hoops and squares; mapping
her daily footpath – its lines and gaps
she skips sideways, her feet stretch

over islands and kingdoms, deserts
and shores. A dictionary opens
behind her ears, spilling furious *fadas*

from the *pócaí* of her coat. A new ache
and a loose tooth, she learns to pare away,
humming her *two by twos* and *four plus fours*.

One April morning in a dash across the room
she lands a blue stone on the art table, the one,
she declares, from her trip round the moon.

REVOLVING TIME
after Ecclesiastes

There is nothing new under the sun
yet behold its rays on the stage of our day,
every inch of its curtain a continuum

all pulled back for the month of June,
audience laughing in late night play;
there is nothing new under the sun,

cacophony of children a familiar tune
a hopscotch of nostalgia to yesterday,
a glimpse through our certain continuum.

The days' long light never needing the moon
but oh the joy of that buck* on the bay,
there is nothing new under the sun.

Ice cream drips from the end of its spoon,
wafered or coned, its taste holds sway
in a swirl of vanilla's continuum.

Autumn nights creeping way too soon
hear the sigh as our days tick away,
for something new under the sun
every ray of its curtain a continuum.

* buck: *referring to the super moon in July described to as the Buck Moon.*

PAUSE

The odd time
an overnight fall
of unexpected snow
catches your breath,
the dawn is held in
a low, slow pause.

Or the sudden howl
of a whipping storm
casts the leaves into
a golden avalanche,
winter suspended
in this reprise.

Such startling days
roll out fresh maps
like blank pages
for the sniffer dog
of the soul to dig
into familiar verges,
for a sure foot
to emerge,

following the pattern
of forward motion
is this your time
to step
            in
                        or
                                    out?

Carmen Cygni

No swan song here, nor at the shoreline where
I fold my fraught wings round you and me
to steady my keel, to hold onto you,
my dreamed of cygnet, and not
hold on to the possibility
of losing you.

You, my promise of life, endangered
in my trickle of bewildering dribs
of blood – has my heart stop
briefly – to listen for the beat of yours.

Through days of fretfulness,
feathered with an urge
I didn't know
I possessed:
an urge so beyond reason,
I barely breathe myself

I wait

for the faint flutter
of you, the tentative
thread I weave to the lilt
and lull of the lake water.

Settle where you belong,
surge to the sway of your own symphony.
Today will hear no swan song.

Stay, nestled inside of me.

THE CUT

In the solitude of the summer garden
a kindful peace drops, peering over the poppies,
the fuchsia, wafting on the paths
where a week ago my daughter, in a pink flowing
dress blended her mix of seed with soil,
sprinkling water on bud and clay; the promise
of blossoms in her parting smile, hugs
postponed until this all ends, her hair a halo
of curly waves, reminiscent of her childhood look
when the war between mother and girl saw her kick
the clay, stomp over any fresh buds, throw
water on the notion of cutting her long mane
of unbrushable knots that hid her eyes, her
face, her pubescent breasts, seedlings
of this woman who now garnishes my salads
with peppery rocket and little gems of May.

A scent of her lives in the notch of my neck –
her teenage peace offering one Mother's Day,
a locket laced with her curls, cut a decade ago,
a souvenir of the battles we choose,
the hurts we save for self, unspoken
words furled in our throats.

Her locks will be cut when the salons reopen,
she'll select her own style and shape,
WhatsApp a shot of her face, reframed.
No matter, I'll wave my white flag of approval,
battle lines long overgrown.
She owns her hair.

LAUDATE
for Charlie Travers

For sixty years he carries psalms in his pockets.
His feet move with the ease of one who has measured
the lightness of his own pace. A bell rings at noon and six
to the rhythm of his trimmings and vespers
while a faint hum trills from his hearing aid.

Eyes that are kind and ever outward
deflect his aging need for a helping hand,
his curved back is more a genuflection.
He reflects my concern with his heed for me.
In alb and surplice, he cloaks me in his faith.

He is the rosary at my grandfather's grave,
the purple stole that calms my mother's leaving,
the consoling hymn across generations of grief.
Through my stained glass woman's heart
he radiates hope as brilliant as the lunula
of the monstrance, so blessed in his hands.

When he presses his palms together in prayer
he is a church spire high above the street.

GOOD FRIDAY 2020

At ninety he stands, present, outside the closed church.
It is 3pm on Good Friday. His stick taps the path three times.

He considers the earth's new Agony in the Garden,
reflects on the words of that green catechism

his boys chanted from, as though in the classroom
they too held the cup from which Jesus had to drink.

Not my will, however, but your will be done.

He bows his head in prayer, a lone man
on the silent street, the town dense with absence.

THE GEOGRAPHY OF A LOST YEAR
"We are closed in, and the key is turned
On our uncertainty."
– W.B. Yeats

When we finally meet, face to face, unveil ourselves
close up, refocus our eyes that spoke for us
these endless months, how will we trace
the new skin of our uncertainty?

Can we manage to unfurl ourselves
for the rays to reflect on our epidermal cells,
shed, layer upon layer,   in the weathering
glare of wearing a mask?

Remember
the touch of another's hand along your cheek,
the tingle of such a tender act, the excitement
and the fear of exposure in reaching out,
getting close to one another?

Relish
in the surround
sound of whispers, vowel shapes
that hear themselves; secrets that can escape,
new stories released and voiced
in the undertones.

Sit
with the thought of your eye
catching the eye of another,
the tang of salt,
of another's breath,
the whiff of garlic,
the crumb on a beard,
the crack in your throat.

Watch
for the faint brush of fine hairs when lips meet,
landmarks in this new space.

Can we allow ourselves to excavate the shape of a smile,
dig out burrowed worry lines and plant our pucker,
light as lipstick, across the scape
of an unmasked mouth?

And what of holding hands, fingers exploring our hidden
places, grooves and curves – unmapped
by another's touch in this
longest of time?

Shaped by this geography of our lost year
unearthed, undone,
uncertainty the only guarantee
between the me that was,
and the me that is.

STITCHES

Some days you find yourself online, hankering for home,
that place you fled, one Sunday, determined and for good.
You put it down to curiosity, your under-the-skin-ness and
half-smile-ness that has her ask, *What's that you're reading?*

At a loss for an answer you return to the life you landed
into on that Monday, the words to articulate goodbye
still packed in the corner of your bedroom wardrobe
hoovered out and well aired the following Friday.

You find yourself feverishly scanning snippets and online
news of the old neighbours: how do you spell out that need
to her, to yourself? Why you wake up every Sunday
clinging to the scent of frankincense from altar boy days?

And on that Tuesday when you read of Doc Frank's death,
the long-gone pain in your leg stabs, and a lonesomeness
for the scent of TCP he used when he deftly stitched you,
needled your shin, despite your longing to leap and run –

as though you could, like
                                        you still think you can.

BRUSH STROKE

This morning you seize the yard brush.
With your one good arm you do
what she would have done,
sweep the street outside your home.

Your head, bent to the task, scratches the surface
of your grief; your one good hand curls around
the handle, imprinted with her fingerprints,
the closest you can get to touching her warmth again.

You recall the months of endless days you lay
recovering in the familiar music of home,
herself coaxing you back from the stroke
that left you half the man she married;

the daily song of the swish and push
of your wife's morning sweep
on the street below your bedroom,
reminding you of where you belong.

She stitched you back with a blanket of comfort,
your healing punctuated by the nods, waves
and words she exchanged with the neighbours
who, like you, thought
she would be the one
sweeping the street before your funeral.

HEARNSBROOK

My father guides us on our weekly gaggle count
and endless choice of gosling names
in our shared ritual –
our daily trip to Hearnsbrook*
my homeplace that unveils itself
as their blessed haven too.

Kneeling, he offers them gifts, like prayers.
In his manger the whiff of leather from the bridles
waits for the next journeyman to saddle up.
Under the reins and collars
still hanging from the roof space
my children, in union with nature and nurture,
are beside themselves with excitement.

His hair another shade of grey, his hands a nest
for these few ounces of downy feathers:
my gentle, coaxing father.

* *Hearnsbrook*: a country farmhouse in Killimor, County Galway

DUST

Loneliness settles round the bed in dust,
on his locker
on his lampshade
on his unused phone
on his unopened books and gifts;

the thumbprint
on the alarm clock
the only sign.

Dust has settled into
the sleeves of the hardbacks
the sleeves of the solitary shirts
shadow dancing in the wardrobe.

An unopened life
tucks itself neatly
beneath the quilt.

He,
a mere ripple
floating from us,
loneliness settles around the bed in dust.

HOMELESS

Sometimes I am noticed –
a blue bundle of pity,
wearing that shade
always suited to my eyes,
the same hue of my first
dancing costume, with its
two strips of Celtic knots,
my eight-year-old curls.
Other times I dream
the drone of the sea
pulling me into the cobalt
of childhood, just there
off the island cliffs
near Gort na gCapall,
the song of the waves as familiar
as today's beat of footsteps.

Or I pray,
wrapped in the warmth
of the Hail Mary, her blue
halo a softening voice
in the blown dust
and clicking heels,
the closed purses
at my eye level.
Sometimes it's Joseph,
the saint's prayer I hold,
propped in my empty cup,
the carpenter who chisels
a crevice to scatter sawdust
there around my childhood feet,
the carver of the welcome door
to the tap of dancers on the floor.

SMITHEREENS

Her heart was bigger than herself
and when it broke

it splintered her kitchen floor,
cracking the black tiles,
shattering the red roof of the turf shed.

Alone this year she carries the load from the bog,
flings her grief into the corner
with each sod

only to see it creep back
like a sleeveen
under the sheets of her half-empty bed

where a year ago in vain
she implored his cradled head
and limp hand, his heart
spent.

LOVE MADE VISIBLE

in an exotic recipe for our breakfast:
oranges, limes, lemons, grapefruit,
the erotic kumquat on the table.

Our two heads lean in, we peel
the outer layers, the knife
deftly cutting strips, fine to coarse,

peelings bed under fingernails,
my flesh smarts from an old cut
as we squeeze the juice,

feel it flow between our fingers,
holding out hands we lick the drips,
then press the last of it into the pan,

wait while pith and pulp and brazen pips
come to the top, steeped in a muslin
sack. In a slow steam

the scents simmer, the punch of rinds
perfumes the house with summer,
clean as fresh bed linen. We'll savour

the bite of Five Fruit Marmalade,
a slow-cooked morning kiss, and us –
a harvest riper than all that fruit.

RETURNING
i.m. Edna O'Brien

On the day they take you home to Iniscealtra,
the lake looks back remembering the gaze of your young eyes
and the gushing flow of your daring imagination;

your townland recalls the ripple of your laughter
and the longing for your purple ink that lingered
long after you fled this place that once was home;

the trees on the shoreline sway, their boughs blessing
today's boat that bears your body to the aloneness
and solitude of the island's moss-lined grave.

Buoyed by your sons' love and a gratitude so deep
it dapples the water so the blue lake rises
to the outpourings of the mourners' grief

and the oars dip to the rhythm and turn of old tunes
that, between breaths, incant a chorus over and over:
she's home, she's home, she's home.

SHIRTS

Flannel

The shirt I once wore
is hanging on your clothesline.
Your wife washed me out.

Linen

A week ago I
pressed the collar of that shirt,
now collared with a rope.

Cotton

You wore this shirt well.
Its threadbare cuffs imprinted
with your aged, still hands.

Silk

I wash then fold it,
the purple shirt you've outgrown
piled with your castoffs.

Denim

That first teenage kiss,
forever young in Levis,
the blue of your eyes.

THE BED

What you share
cannot be undone by age
or sorrow.
– Lisa C. Taylor, 'What Lovers Know'

Like a pair of undertakers
two strong strangers lift with ease
this chart of my long-ended marriage,

carry it through the bedroom door;
stagnant motes of detritus and dander
flying with skin and hair,

the scent of thirty years
swallowed by the springs,

the imprint of estranged lovers
shoved out the door,

leavings of anger rise
in the heartquake of betrayal.

My new bed fits the empty place,
a blessing in this measured space,

let him off,
no payback,
no looking back.

What Consent Looks Like

You watch the clothesline
dance itself around your body,
circling the afterplay of unwelcome sex;

you chase the runaway stockings
trying to find a hint
of last night's wetness;

the ladder in the sheer 10-denier
a guilty reminder
of the uninvited fingers

that made their way inside
the *rich amber* nylon,
rolling your vowels

from *wrong* to *right*,
no to *yes*;

you wring the sleeves
of your white shorn shirt,
stained

to a self-conscious shame,
like the hollow cups
of your castaway bra.

STRIPPED CLEAR AGAINST THE SKY*

It's what happens after autumn lures the leaves
into a reminder that every self

will be stripped bare, each hair and cell, each
branch and twig. And it's what happens

under the wolf moon
in full view, clear against the sky,

reaching in, touching the dark fear of dying.
When winter wipes the window

and the moon shapes your face in a reflection of itself
to you
to me
it's what happens.

* The title is a phrase from *Winter Branches* by Margaret Widdemer

Nothing
doing
alone
I am.
Forlorn,
apprehensive,
black and
ice white
all around.

Around all
white ice
and black,
apprehensive
forlorn.
Am I
alone
doing
nothing?

MURMURATION OVER LOUGH DERG
"My heart in hiding
Stirred for a bird"
– Gerard Manley Hopkins

From out of the ordinary, at the lowest light
of the year on the holiest days of souls and saints,
the indigo canvas a backdrop for the calligraphy
of sky ballet where the Shannon greets the lake,

a choreography

                                        of feathers

            curlicued
                    and curl
    ing,
                            ebb and
                                    sweep   fast
        then   slow,
            sink
                            low
            swish
                                    dive,   rise
                                            deep
                                                    hold
in a high arabesque
then
                dip
                drop
                            into callow and reed;
        a final rush,
the sky,
        in an orchestra of wings
                            draws the curtain
                                        whoosh
            on this November blue.

THE MAGI OF BEARA
i.m. John Eagle

The landscape made a hard walk of it
for the long line of mourners
descending in threes and fours

from places like Ardgroom and Adrigole,
adding to the numbers of neighbours,
and his only brother, waiting.

Under shoals of stars at the mortuary
in Harrington's, the fishermen
and seafarers, cured with sea salt

tacked themselves alongside farmers;
shopkeepers and writers lined the one room
to pay respect to him, the photographer

whose soul was keened as far as Ardnakinna
lighthouse where his lens once zoomed, his brush
catching every shade of blue, cascade and river.

The rows of creviced faces, palms like coarse
spades calloused from the copper of the mines
scoop the hands of those who sat in line

to meet the sympathisers for his sake.
From Allihies and Eyeries. through the hungry hills
they came – the Magi of Beara to his December wake.

ENDPOINT

Cradling the set square she came across
buried in a basket of random things,
she traces her dead son's dotted initials, barely
able to handle this sharp-edged souvenir.

Two rays with the same endpoint is an angle.

In his one mistake, disorientated perhaps,
he misjudged his angle, miscalculated
the width, misread the height, falling
to death ... a dot in the city's night.

A point is a location in space represented by a dot.

Compass missing, protractor still
in his *Helix Oxford* where his solutions
to problems of geometry were resolved
in a language he found simple to translate.

A space extends infinitely in all directions
and is a set of all points in three dimensions.

She can almost smell him, see his shape
almost, the curve of his neck bent to draw
the line, concise and straight. This end
line her grief will never comprehend.

A line is a collection of points that extend forever.

JASMINE IN JANUARY

After the expectant days of Christmas
a belated gift surprises.
Labelled *Jasmine & Joy*
the aroma from its decorative tin
jolts the dull grey of January
and I am away,
sent by this bouquet
across oceans and stars, inhaling
the morning air in Grasse,
heady with its own frisson
in the bustle of its July harvest.

No wonder the tanners infused the royal leather gloves
with the magic of jasmine; no wonder
they took such pride in the grandiflorum picked at dawn
when the scent is at its most intense.

Harvested by hand in daily matins,
so many petals are plucked painstakingly
for a yield of one kilo takes 8000 flowers,
so many fingers, so many hands.

Skimming my middle finger across
the smooth skin of the body cream,
velvety as butter, I savour the infusion
of flowers, of warmth and all
those generations of hands, century
after century, that gather
and harvest this bountiful earth.

And I thank my benefactor
for the journey he gifted me
in January.

SILENCE OF STONE
Portumna Workhouse, County Galway

My history's here in the silence of stone,
life story echoed in whispers of wood,
hear my voice ring from the ivy and weeds.
In the rustle of hawthorn, oak and beech

my life story echoes in whispers of wood
where ghost children play, cold and forlorn.
Here in the rustle of hawthorn and beech
I gave shelter and food under my roof,

where my ghost children play, cold and forlorn,
trace out the boards where they curled on the straw.
Here they found shelter under my roof,
wove cobwebs on beams that still hold their dreams.

Trace out the boards where they curled on the straw
and open my doors, leave all stigma behind,
clear the beams' webs that captured their dreams,
pull down my gates, let the outside in.

Fling open my doors, leave my stigma behind.
Here, my voice sings through the ivy and weeds,
swing back my gates, let the curious in –
my history is heard in the silence of stone.

THE RAFTERS AT PORTUMNA WORKHOUSE

Outside the high walls
of whitewash and chalk

a trembling hand
slips into mine,

a slender parcel
of skin and pulse

seeking my heat,
drawing me

through the heavy door
with its daunting black key

to a winter of flagstones.

In faith we climb
the timber stairs

hand in hand.
I unfold our fingers

to the surprise
of a sickle wing

– here
then gone –

a swift rising
to the rafters.

To the fading
of a child's footsteps,

a whoosh of feathers
settles in the caul of stone.

ALEXIS SOYER'S SIX MINUTE SOUP*
*after Kieran Tuohy***

I peel a white onion,
measure handfuls of pearl barley,
bones from the butcher's block,
melt the dripping for Soyer's recipe
once used to stave off starvation
in the soup kitchens of Ireland.

Alexis Soyer wore a French beret,
his *Pâté de pithiviers*
laced Queen Victoria's coronation.
From his *Shilling Cookery* book
I'm adapting the one hundred gallon
recipe for my soup pot.

I add celery, leeks and turnip,
a light scatter of white flour,
glugs of water, and just enough
salt as would fill the head
of a haw. I stir the lot,
let it simmer for hours.

A quart of broth sits
in my soup bowl, grey and insipid.
And now I see them, the ragged
clawing for some seldom food
here in my warm kitchen;
the workhouse wretched
dragging themselves in zigzag

lines, past the check clerk,
the indicator recording numbers:
a hundred bellies every six minutes.
In one hour Soyer's soup slaked
the want of a thousand of our living dead.

The pot is roiling.
I peal the bell to move them on.

* Alexis Soyer: a French chef who moved to Britain where he was chef of the Reform Club and was known to have prepared breakfast for Queen Victoria. He requested and was sent to set up his soup kitchen in Dublin in 1847.

** Kieran Tuohy: Sculptor of the Dark Shadows exhibition of bog oak sculptures at the Irish Workhouse Centre, Portumna. One of his pieces is a bell of bog oak. This piece is titled *The Six Minute Soup*.

JARS FROM A GHETTO
i.m. Irena Sendler (15 February 1910–12 May 2008)
nom de guerre: Jolanta

Because you found yourself alone in your dark country,
resonant with your father's words; words that willed you
strength to toss a lifebuoy over Warsaw's raging waters,

you saved the drowning in their ghettoed waiting zones.
The too many faces, born under a different star, cast
to the turbulence of Treblinka imprinted on your memory.

Each new name you record alongside the name bestowed
by parents they may never see again. Inscribed on strips
of tissue you add the matching address of their new home.

Like a gardener sowing seeds, you bury these secrets
in glass jars opposite the Gestapo barracks, beneath
the apple tree – old and new identities, underground.

No one ever told, though they tried to squeeze
your memory, stamped you with the death penalty.
Thankfully, for those recorded names that needed you,

you were released to free the names and jars.
An *ordinary thing* you say you did, though haunted
by the moments, where the price of parting was grief.

At night when you don't sleep you see their eyes, recall
their grappling hands, bony fingers that unlace themselves
from the ghetto to a safer life,

and you lament you could not save the others,
the ones buried in the shadowed landscape
of your fear-filled dreams.

On the anniversary of your death
our snow-globe shakes in the tremor of today's savagery.
For those of us far less heroic, we have to believe

somewhere,
rising from their restlessness,
there is another Jolanta.

WÜRFELZUCKER

I

Germany 1921/2021

I picture her, the German grandmother
you inherited your smile from,
your sweet tooth,
a carrier, a collector
of würfelzucker, its perfect size
slipping into her glove
or up her sleeve –
enveloped cubes of sweetness
too perfectly wrapped
to leave behind,
too scarce to dip
into her kaffee glass.
A taste
appreciated
all the more after the war
stored in the tin she bequeathed to you,
repurposed in another country
she'd never heard of,
where syllables of würfelzucker
roll themselves
on a foreign tongue
like a poem.

II

Churchill War Rooms 1945/1980

In a map room in 1945, a British Wing Commander
shaved slivers of sweetness into daily infusions of tea,
his rationed cubes hoarded in the depths of his desk drawer.

Forty years on, the drawer reveals a stash of three
intact sugar cubes that survived the decades
stowed in a blue envelope, labelled *John Heagerty*,

the pilot who manned the room's maps, the scanner
of the skies he had once flown for the RAF
before the Red Baron grounded him to desk duty.

On 8 May 1945 I imagine him rush out for air,
abandoning his secret stash, his three cubes
for a cluster of white clouds.

III

Moravia 1841/2024

In 1841 a delighted Jacob Rad dashed out, heading home
from his sugar refinery, carrying a cardboard box. Over
devoted nights and days calculating and pressing, he
designed and compressed to perfection his gift of three
hundred and fifty five cubes. He presented the sweetness
of pink and white into his Julianna's hands. When he
became aware of her fingers sliced and scarred by the knife
she'd needed to hack the grains from the sugar loaf, her
pain became his pain. Oh to have witnessed her eyes
behold his, the surprise melt of that first ever sugar cube
on her lips and tongue. Watch too the curiosity of tourists
trekking the Moravian Mountains today. Stirring espressos
at a small café in Dačice, they notice the cuboid monument
placed in memory of famous Jacob Rad. Balancing yet
teetering on just one vertex, from a pedestal of granite, one
precise white cube is

     propped,
         ready
            to
                diss
                    ol
                        v
                            e

TEORA*

Locked in a world of pills and syringes
the door closed to familiar faces,
the behind the counter transformed,
fronted by a screen to the outside world,
the cologne of Yardley and Lancôme
overthrown by the sanitised scent
of methylated spirits and absolute alcohol.

The busy dispensary of banter and chat
is reduced to labels and printers, phones
and panic. The rows of luscious lipsticks
abandoned, lips disappear behind masks.
The urgency of the day rings in my ears
into the night, revisiting and revision
of guidelines and protocols
roiling in turmoiled dream.

Then driving out to Bridie's house
in the early May evening light,
from over the lake a lone heron
takes itself into the air
with barely a flap ... and I wonder
was it for Bridie's prescription alone
that I find myself
on the road to Loughatorick.**

Teora: border or boundary
Loughatorick: so called as the boundary line between County Galway
and County Clare runs through the lake.

THE VOICE KEEPER

For twenty years and more
her room on the Mall echoes
with the timbre of boy sopranos
in rows of promise beside her piano.

She is the moon on the tide of their breath,
drawing the faltering airs, holding
each phrase with care until she
shapes their whisper
into song,

into tunes that are swept
along the streetscape,
up to the high steeple,
warbles that pipe their way
to the row of horse chestnuts
in their standing ovation
to the keeper who knows the rise
and fall of every phase,
its waxing and waning
like a traditional slow air.

The Road to New Inn

On Thursdays, the day for New Inn,
with imperfect perfection my trio pours into the car,
violin, viola and cello in a weekly divining
at the musical well.

Our overture plays out on the road, punctuated
with white lines through villages
that hold dynamics of their own.
Legato on the first stretch,
a minor chord hits in Killimor,
tractors always slowing the pace.

As we pass harmonic Hearnsbrook
a *crescendo* builds
approaching the graceful waltz
that is Gortymadden.

Here, a change of key
to the metronome
of my indicator – we turn right
and hit a major 7th at Mullagh,
a page turn at the crossroad.

Stacatto. Yield.
Then straight ahead,
the back seat full of shrills and high-pitched cymbals
watching for the dog who's always chasing his tail
outside the shop,
the grace note and treat stop
at Cappataggle Cross.

And if
carried away
by the arpeggios of Máirtín O'Connor's *Road West*,

fingers dancing on the steering wheel, my pace quickening
with the maestro's finger work, volume up to drown
the groans of reluctance from the highly-strung daughters,
my car might end up in the dead march of Kilconnell
where a *scherzo* is needed to make it on time.

Pedal and foot sharpened to the *pizzicato*
of the engine, the windscreen
rosined by the wipers,
we arrive with the rain at New Inn, the end of the line.

Moods, music and hormones
in a *glissando* of girls
glide from my car,
sometimes practised,
rarely polished –
in a mad dash to the *seomra ceoil*.

Acknowledgements

Thanks to the editors of the following publications where versions of these poems first appeared: *Boyne Berries, Crannóg, Drawn to the Light,* RTÉ *Sunday Miscellany, Live Encounters, Local Wonders* (Dedalus), *Romance Options* (Dedalus), *Scríobh* (Niland 2006), *Skylight 47, Staying Human* (Bloodaxe*), Strokestown Poetry* anthologies, *the Irish Times, Washing Windows* anthologies (Arlen House).

Gratitude to:
Alan Hayes of Arlen House for his belief in my writing. It is an honour to be published in the 50th year of this highly-regarded publishing house.

Geraldine Mills for her poetic sensibility and in-depth advice.

My fellow Portumna Pen Pushers: Marie Barrett, Barbara Kennedy (RIP), Declan Burke-Kennedy (RIP), Kevin Chesser, Joe Conmy, Gerry Davis (RIP), Anne Deroe, Anna Dillon, Patricia Donnellan, Wiltrud Dull, Margaret Hickey, Anthony Lenihan, Peter Martin, Maureen Moss, Conor McAnally, Monique McGuinness, Mary Rourke, Elizabeth Ryan and Eileen Smith.

At the University of Limerick: Emily Cullen, Eoin Devereaux, Sarah Moore-Fitzgerald, Donal Ryan and Joseph O'Connor for encouraging the flow of my words.

Peers: Gerardine Burke, Patrick Chapman, Shauna Gilligan, Margaret Hickey, Sara Mullen, Mari Maxwell, Lucy McCrann, Nuala O'Connor and Tony O'Dwyer.

My fellow creative and writerly friends: Deirdre Devally, Ger Fahy, Brendan Flynn, Sue Booth-Forbes, Peggie Gallagher, Betty Gough, Vona Groarke, Christine Guillen, Gerard Hanberry, Thomas McCarthy, Alan McMonagle, Geraldine McNulty, Geraldine Mitchell, Luke Morgan, Róisín O'Brien,

Anne O'Leary, Eileen O'Donoghue, Pippa Slattery, Ruth Smith, Lisa C. Taylor, Josephine Vahey.

Festivals and spaces that provide platforms: Baffle Poetry (Loughrea); Dromineer-Nenagh Literary Festival; Galway City Library; Lime Square Poets; Maple Poetry Group (Portumna); Roscommon New Writing, Shorelines Arts Festival; SiarScéal; Strokestown International Poetry Festival; Portumna Library and the Irish Workhouse Centre, Portumna.

Poetry Ireland for honouring me as Strokestown's Poet Laureate in 2021 as part of their Poetry Towns project.

Máire Ní Dhuibhir for setting my work to music in *Stepping Stones* (2024).

Liz Kelly for inclusion of my words on Portumna's Galway 2020 sphere.

My teachers, Sr Brigid Feeney (RIP) and Jim Gibbons (RIP) who instilled and nurtured my interest in poetry.

My siblings, Carmel, Brenda and Shane who all share in the music of life, words and dance that flows through our Morrison and Lynskey genes.

My daughters, Ailbhe, Orla and Máirín who have put up with my poetic musings all their lives, and to Síofra, my muse. Buíochas agus grá.

ABOUT THE AUTHOR

A native of Strokestown, County Roscommon, and living in Portumna, County Galway, Noelle Lynskey completed an MA in Creative Writing at the University of Limerick in 2022. She was selected by Poetry Ireland as Strokestown's Poet Laureate in 2021. She was also commissioned by Galway City Library in 2021 to collaborate with musician Ger Fahy in the project, *1921 Dialogue through Poetry and Music.* She has collaborated on a series of writing workshops with Gerard Hanberry at the Irish Workhouse Centre under the umbrella of Creative Ireland. Noelle has judged various poetry competitions and was commissioned in September 2024 to facilitate a series of workshops to celebrate Portumna Library. With multiple awards and readings to her name Noelle's writing is featured in numerous anthologies and broadcast widely. She facilitates Portumna Pen Pushers and is artistic adviser to Shorelines Arts Festival, having directed the festival for fifteen years. Poetry has been a passion all her life; publishing her first poem in a magazine called *Kairos* when she was 16 years old, and her pen has not stopped since. A mother of three adult daughters, and a community pharmacist, Noelle draws from the well of mothering, womanhood and life's journey within a rural community. She is truly delighted to launch her debut collection of poems that span over five decades.